Welcome!
THIS BOOK'S FOR YOU.

Every page, every picture, and
every word was designed for
your pleasure.

Lucky, lucky reader.
BE GLAD IT'S NOT 1726.

BACK THEN, CHILDREN HAD TO READ
preachy poems and fables,
religious texts that made them fear that death was
near, and manuals that told them where to stand,
how to sit, not to laugh, and scores of other rules.

Because the
future champion
OF CHILDREN'S BOOKS
was just a lad.

—

bal·der·dash *noun:* nonsense, poppycock,
malarkey, moonshine, flummery, or bunk

BALDERDASH!

To every librarian who has assisted me on my projects,
including those in Special Collections, for getting those tiny,
wonderful antique books into my hands —M. M.

In memory of Vinnie Kralyevich—whose mind bubbled with ideas —N. C.

This edition published exclusively for KiwiCo in 2021 by Chronicle Books LLC.
Originally published in hardcover in 2017 by Chronicle Books LLC.

Library of Congress Cataloging-in-Publication Data available
under the original edition ISBN 978-0-8118-7922-4.

ISBN 978-1-7972-1766-6

Manufactured in China.

Design by Kristine Brogno.
Typeset in Old Claude, Veneer, and Zapatista.
The illustrations in this book were rendered
in pen and ink and digital media.

10 9 8 7 6 5 4 3 2 1

Chronicle Books LLC
680 Second Street
San Francisco, California 94107

Chronicle Books—we see things differently.
Become part of our community at www.chroniclekids.com.

BALDERDASH!

John Newbery and the Boisterous Birth of Children's Books

Written by MICHELLE MARKEL * Illustrated by NANCY CARPENTER

chronicle books · san francisco

WELCOME!

THIS BOOK'S FOR YOU.

Every page,
    every picture,
    every word, and even its
        letters are designed for
        your pleasure.

Lucky, lucky reader.
BE GLAD IT'S NOT 1726.

In those days of powdered wigs and petticoats, England was brimming with books. Books of pirates and monsters and miniature people. Tales of travels and quests and shipwrecks and crimes. At the fairs, in the market stalls, in the bookshop windows were hundreds of wonderful books.

But not for children.

Oh, no.

CHILDREN HAD TO READ

preachy poems and fables,

religious texts that made them fear that death was near,
and manuals that told them where to stand,
how to sit,
not to laugh,
and scores of other rules.

Because the
future champion
OF CHILDREN'S BOOKS
was just a lad.

HIS NAME WAS
John Newbery.

The boy lived on a farm but fancied reading more than forking hay, so upon coming of age, he set off to work for a printer.

John got a kick out of

TYPE STICKS AND TYPE STANDS AND CHASES AND QUOINS.

He came to love galleys and presses and the smell of fresh ink.

As soon as he was able, **John became a publisher himself.**

Then he went big time—he moved to

London,
CENTER OF THE BOOKSELLING TRADE.

LONDON BRIDGE

Smack dab in the heart of the book marketplace,
in St. Paul's Churchyard,
he found a place for a store.
Brilliant!
The streets were bustling with tradesmen, doctors,
lawyers, clerks, and many other eager readers.

John wanted to publish fine books for the whole lot of them—and for their children. He knew the youngsters were hungry for stories. Many boys and girls handed coppers to street hawkers for ugly chapbooks of fairy tales, or for chopped-up versions of grown-up books.

JOHN LIKED CHILDREN.

Why shouldn't they have

delightful

books of their own?

John! What were you thinking!

What about the parents? Many mums and dads worried
that if their little nippers read fun books, they'd turn
wild as savages!

BALDERD
I agree.
Reading should be a treat for children.
John Locke 1632-170

Reading should be a treat for children.

That's what a famous philosopher wrote, and John agreed.

So did two other publishers. One issued a book with alphabet rhymes and well-known stories, and the other printed itty-bitty books about animals, plants, and local buildings.

John wanted his first book for children to be **irresistible.** There'd be letters from Jack the Giant-Killer.

There'd be pictures of

PITCH AND HUSSEL, HOOP AND HIDE, **blindman's buff,**

and other children's games.

Plus
ABC's,
PROVERBS,
and other classic material,
and for extra punch—
A MESSAGE TO MUMS AND DADS.

He ordered gilt floral paper for the covers, and titled his creation *A LITTLE PRETTY POCKET-BOOK.*

"Price of book alone, 6 pence, with a ball or pincushion, 8 pence," the notice read.

A BOOK AND TOY! WHY HADN'T ANYONE ELSE THOUGHT OF THAT?

Then John set his bright books in the window of his store, and wondered, **Will the parents buy them? Are they too . . . cheerful?**

The children
gobbled them
up like plum cakes.

John thought if they liked fun, attractive books, they'd probably like a magazine, too. Grown-ups read magazines—why shouldn't children?

A MAGAZINE WITH rhymes, riddles, recipes, stories.

Adorned with crisp copperplate engravings.

Working in the back of his bookshop, or chatting with his chums in the tavern, John's mind bubbled with more ideas. For older children, he printed books about arithmetic, geography, astronomy, and other subjects—including one taught by a pretend boy philosopher named Tom Telescope.

Then John came up with his most ingenious product for youngsters yet. A novel! Grown-ups were reading novels, why shouldn't the little masters and ladies? One long, luscious story to savor for several days.

THE HISTORY OF LITTLE GOODY TWO-SHOES

is about a raggedy orphan who is left to wander the roads.

Despite many misfortunes, the girl betters herself. She carves her own alphabet blocks and teaches poor children.

She strolls around with a dog, a lamb, and various birds that she has rescued and educated (Ralph, her pet raven, even writes poems).

Two shoes!

Though she starts off penniless, Goody ends up marrying a country squire rich enough to own a coach and six.

A coach and six! In those days, that was like riding in a luxury car. Goody went from rags to riches without a fairy godmother. She did it through study, hard work, and kindness. You can too, the book was saying. And John believed it.

GOODY TWO-SHOES became a smash hit, both in England and across the ocean, in America.

TO THIS DAY, ITS AUTHOR IS A MYSTERY.

All the books John published for his "little friends," as he called
the young readers, were written anonymously or by people with
silly, made-up names.

Another of John's books was about a tumultuous fair, and
its dedication was signed "you know who."

But everyone knew who.
Who else had a shop that sold
ABC books,
GIFT BOOKS,
books about Tom Thumb
AND GILES GINGERBREAD,
books of jokes and riddles,
BOOKS OF SCIENCE, HISTORY,
AND GEOGRAPHY,
that were loved so hard,
that were thumbed so often,
they came apart at the spine?

Who else sold thousands of copies, inspiring other publishers to start making delightful books for young people?

JOHN NEWBERY,
the father of children's literature.
Huzza!

The
Grand Design
in the
Nurture of Children,
is to make them

STRONG,
HARDY,
HEALTHY,
VIRTUOUS,
WISE,
and
HAPPY.

—JOHN NEWBERY,
FROM *A LITTLE
PRETTY POCKET-BOOK*

John Newbery learned publishing—as well as shop keeping—by working as an assistant to William Carnan in the city of Reading. Carnan published a newspaper called *The Reading Mercury* and ran a store that sold medicines and other wares. Upon his death, Newbery inherited a share of the business. Two years later, Newbery married Carnan's widow, Mary, and became stepfather to her three children. Later, they had three children of their own.

Newbery began publishing newspapers and books for adults while living in Reading and continued to do so after moving to London. Noted authors Oliver Goldsmith, Christopher Smart, and Samuel Johnson wrote for his adult publications, and may have penned some of his children's books.

Newbery's books for children were approximately 4 inches by 3 inches (10 centimetres by 7.5 centimetres), which made them easily portable in pockets. He published more than one hundred books for children over his lifetime, and sold thousands of copies, establishing both the value and popularity of books written, illustrated, designed, and printed especially for the perspectives and enthusiasms of children.

Along with books, Newbery sold a patented medicine called Dr. James's Fever Powder, and he came up with clever ways of advertising both books and medicine. He ran ads in newspapers and had characters mention his products inside his books—Woglog the Giant was a villain in a story in Newbery's *Lilliputian Magazine,* but later, in Newbery's *Fables in Verse,* Woglog changes his bad ways and steps civilly into a bookstore to read some of "Mr. Newbery's little books." At the beginning of *The History of Little Goody Two-Shoes,* Margery's father dies because he was "seized with a violent fever in a place where Dr. James's powder was not to be had." When Margery becomes a tutor, she sings a song from Newbery's *The Little Pretty Plaything,* teaches at a school run by a character from *Nurse Truelove's New-Year's Gift,* and her students read books sold at the Bible and Sun (Newbery's bookshop).

Twenty years before Newbery was born, noted philosopher John Locke wrote a popular treatise called *Some Thoughts Concerning Education.* He believed that it was important for children to have healthy bodies, strong moral character, and the right choice of learning materials, including "easy and pleasant books."

Locke's ideas may have influenced two publishers who made lighthearted, illustrated books for children shortly before Newbery: Thomas Boreman issued a series of miniature books on plants, animals, and landmarks between 1740 and 1743, and Thomas Cooper published his ABC miscellany in 1742. Cooper's wife, Mary, published the very first collection of nursery rhymes two years later, around the same time that Newbery's *A Little Pretty Pocket-Book* appeared.

One hundred fifty-five years after Newbery lived, the American Library Association created the very first children's book award in the world and named it after John Newbery. It is given annually to "the most distinguished contribution to American literature for children" to this day.

THE BOOKS MENTIONED IN THIS BOOK

In *A Little Pretty Pocket-Book,* Jack the Giant-Killer addresses his letters to Little Master Tommy and Pretty Miss Polly, two fictitious children. Jack explains how the ball and cushion could be used to monitor their conduct: every time the children were good, their nurse could put a pin on the red side of the ball or cushion, and when they were bad, on the black side. When ten pins were used up, the youngsters could be rewarded or punished, accordingly.

The main character of *The History of Little Goody Two-Shoes* is named Margery Meanwell. After the death of her parents, she becomes so poor she has only one shoe. When a kind gentleman buys her a new pair, she exclaims "see my two shoes" to everyone she meets, and acquires the nickname "Goody Two-Shoes." "Goody," short for "goodwife," was a polite form of addressing women in that era (we now use Miss, Mrs., or Ms.). As time went by, the term "goody two-shoes" came to describe someone who behaves well in order to attract attention.

In *The History of Giles Gingerbread,* a baker teaches his son Giles how to read by making letters and books out of gingerbread.

See here's little Giles,
With his Gingerbread book,
For which he doth long,
And at which he doth look;
Till by longing and looking,
He gets it by heart,
And then eats it up,
As we eat up a tart.

Giles and his dad, like several of Newbery's characters, reappear in later books. In Newbery's book about a fair, *The Fairing,* they hawk gingerbread "wives" and "husbands" from a stall.

The Circle of the Sciences came in several volumes and covered spelling, grammar, arithmetic, rhetoric, poetry, logic, geography, and chronology. It could be considered the first children's encyclopedia.

In *The Newtonian System of Philosophy Adapted to the Capacities of Young Gentlemen and Ladies,* a boy philosopher named Tom Telescope gives lectures on the natural sciences, using toys and other familiar objects.

FURTHER READING

Granahan, Shirley. *John Newbery: Father of Children's Literature.* Edina, MN: Publishing Pioneers, 2009.

History of Making Books, The: From Clay Tablets, Papyrus Rolls, and Illuminated Manuscripts to the Printing Press. New York: Scholastic, 1996.

Roberts, Russell. *John Newbery and the Story of the Newbery Medal.* Hockessin, DE: Mitchell Lane Publishers, 2004.

SELECTED BIBLIOGRAPHY

Alderson, Brian, and Felix de Marez Oyens. *Be Merry and Wise: Origins of Children's Book Publishing in England,* 1650–1850. London: British Library, 2006.

Avery, Gillian, and Briggs, Julia, eds, *Children and Their Books, a Celebration of the Work of Iona and Peter Opie.* Oxford: Clarendon Press, 1989.

Darton, F. J. Harvey. *Children's Books in England.* 3rd ed. Rev. Brian Alderson. Cambridge: Cambridge University Press, 1932.

Gillespie, John T., and Corinne J. Naden. The Newbery Companion: *Booktalk and Related Materials for Newbery and Honors Books.* Englewood, CO: Libraries Unlimited, 1996.

Hunt, Peter, and Dennis Butts, et al. *Children's Literature: An Illustrated History*. Oxford: Oxford University Press, 1995.

Kernan, Alvin B. *Printing Technology, Letters, and Samuel Johnson*. Princeton, NJ: Princeton University Press, 1987.

Roscoe, Sydney. *John Newbery and His Successors, 1740–1814*. Wormley, Hertfordshire: Five Owls Press, 1973.

Thwaite, M.F. *From Primer to Pleasure: An Introduction to the History of Children's Books in England, from the Invention of Printing to 1900*. London: Library Association, 1963.

Townsend, John Rowe. *John Newbery and His Books: Trade and Plumb-Cake for Ever, Huzza!* Metuchen, NJ: Scarecrow Press, 1994.

Welsh, Charles. *A Bookseller of the Last Century: Being Some Account of the Life of John Newbery*. Clifton, N.J. Augustus M. Kelley, 1972.

ARTICLES

Bator, Robert. "Out of the Ordinary Road: John Locke and English Juvenile Fiction in the Eighteenth Century." *Children's Literature* 1 (1972): 46–53.

Brown, Gillian. "The Metamorphic Book: Children's Print Culture in the Eighteenth Century." *Eighteenth-Century Studies* 39.3 (Spring 2006): 351–362.

Hewins, C. M. "The History of Children's Books" *The Atlantic* (January 1888). Web. 3 January 2009.

Morgenstern, John. "The Rise of Children's Literature Reconsidered." *Children's Literature Association Quarterly* 26.2 (Summer 2001): 64–73.

O'Malley, Andrew. "The Coach and Six: Chapbook Residue in Late Eighteenth-Century Children's Literature." *The Lion and the Unicorn* 24.1 (January 2000): 18–44.

"Printing Press." *Citizendium: The Citizen's Compendium*. Web. 2 May 2009.

Schiller, Justin G. "Artistic Awareness in Early Children's Books." *Children's Literature* 3 (1974): 177–185.